DEVOTIONS,
ADVICE & RENEWAL
for when
Motherhood
FEELS TOO HARD

DEVOTIONS, ADVICE & RENEWAL

for when

Motherhood FEELS TOO HARD

Kelly Crawford

From the author...

Dear Mother,

If you are tired, if you feel alone, if you feel overwhelmed, this book is for you.

Take a deep breath. Understand that you are not alone, and that your feelings do not make you a bad mother, or an inadequate mother. You haven't "messed up" by having children or choosing motherhood.

Years ago mothers lived in a different culture. One that affirmed their position of supreme importance, thereby bolstering their strength for those hard days—hard years—when they were in the thick of battling for their homes and the hearts and souls of their children. Mothers, aunts, grandmothers, and friends banded together in the unifying belief that mother-work was good work, hard as it is, and worth every ounce of ourselves.

But now things are different. Our culture disdains motherhood, and mothers often find themselves feeling like an island in an ocean of scoffers. This loneliness can become unbearable when the hard days press in.

And who can she tell? It's "her fault" after all for choosing full-time motherhood when she could have chosen something more "meaningful". That is the message she's been given.

But you are about to embark on a journey of hope, renewal, and regeneration in your calling of motherhood.

Motherhood is still of supreme importance; it is the lifeblood of our society, a sacred calling given to you by your Creator. And for that reason, we mothers must win the race, believing that He is faithful Who has called us to this task.

This book is meant to be your companion, breathing life back into your mission. Keep it close. There is one entry for each day of the month. Meditate on the message, and ask the Lord to help the words come alive in your life. May the God of hope fill you with all joy and peace in believing, so that by the power of the Holy Spirit you may abound in hope. Romans 15:13.

Through the Watches of the Night

Kristyn Getty

I look towards the wintering trees
To hush my fretful soul
As they rise to face the icy sky
And hold fast beneath the snow.
Their rings grow wide, their roots go deep
That they might hold their height
And stand like valiant soldiers
Through the watches of the night.

No human shoulder ever bears
The weight of all the world
But hearts can sink beneath the ache
Of trouble's sudden surge.
Yet far beyond full knowing
There's a strong unsleeping light
That reaches round to hold me
Through the watches of the night.

I have cried upon the steps that seem
Too steep for me to climb

And I've prayed against a burden
I did not want to be mine.
But here I am and this is where
You're calling me to fight
And You I will remember
Through the watches of the night . . .
You I will remember
Through the watches of the night.

DAY 2

Moses, Motherhood and the Beauty of Broken Vessels

It was a simple prayer . . . *but I couldn't stop sobbing.*

During church this morning, during intercessory prayer—just like every Sunday, a prayer was offered up for the expecting moms in our church, of which I am one.

The prayer went something like, *"Thank you, Lord, for the incredible gift of immortal souls whom you have given us to bring up to love You."*

At that moment, the weight of my responsibility met with my overwhelming feelings of inadequacy, and I began to sob.

"It's too big, Lord . . . it's too hard," were the silent cries of my heart.

And as unexpectedly as the tears came His voice . . . "Remember Moses".

I flipped through my Bible after the prayer, and scanned through the call to Moses in Exodus to rescue God's people from Egypt.

Moses pleaded with God three times—even while beholding the miracle of the burning bush—that he was not capable.

The first time he said . . . *"Who am I?"* (3:11)

The second time he said . . . *"But they will not believe me or listen to me."* (4:1)

The third time (can you imagine his desperation?) . . . *"I can't even talk right!"* (4:10)

And God's answer to Moses was, "Certainly I will be with you."

God doesn't call perfect people to do His work (praise Him!).

He chooses the broken, the imperfect, the weak, so that His power can be revealed. ("Therefore I will glory in my infirmities, for when I am weak, You are strong.")

And God says to this mother, and to you . . . "Certainly I will be with You."

Most definitely. You can be sure of it.

I do feel, as Moses must have, that my task is too much sometimes. And God knew the task was too much for Moses . . . if Moses were given it to do alone.

But God said to Moses . . . "I AM that I AM."

And He is for us . . .

All He wants—all He has ever wanted is a willing, obedient heart. That is the only vessel through which He can show forth His power.

> "Father, make me a willing vessel, broken as I am, through which You demonstrate Yourself to the world."

Humility is the secret, the paradox of the Christian life, that gives us supernatural strength, serenity and peace. It was when the Lord brought me to my lowest point and showed me that pride was a blaring sin in my life that repentance brought the beginning of healing. Repentance, I say, is key. Unconfessed sin, stubborn refusal to root it out depresses and makes sick the Christian soul. Trying, in my own effort is pride. Irritations because things aren't going "my way", instead of a sincere concern for the hearts of my children is pride. Humility is simply emptying ourselves so that He can fill us up. It is the realization that we are nothing. It is solely "being about my Father's business", undaunted by the praises or criticisms of men and concerned only with living a life unto Him. This is the secret to peace and strength.

Warrior Mother

She smiled at me with a knowing glance. *"You are on the front lines..."* my dear friend said to me as I sat crying softly beside her.

Do you ever feel overwhelmed? Inadequate? I do. I have had plenty of "throwing up hands" and feelings of desperation.

I've also learned a lot about the benefits of feeling inadequate, of knowing "this job is too big for me". Because at the moment we think we are able in our own strength, we become *useless for the Kingdom.*

My prayer for you is a prayer for myself. Cry if you need to cry. And then run to Him Who is ready to give you rest.

> My Father, give us a sturdiness of mind and heart for the many tasks ahead.
>
> May we speak with the law of kindness on our tongues. Make us helpers, suitable for our husbands—forgetting our selfish wants, and truly looking to lighten his load.

May we be a crown to him, and not rotten-ness in his bones. Give us strength of body to build this house and not tear it down.

Adorn us with the ornament of a meek and quiet spirit. Make us long suffering toward our husbands and children, not easily provoked and not easily provoking to anger.

Give us energy and vision to "watch over the affairs of our households", seeing it through Your eyes...a mission field, and a battleground to be won for You. Help us speak with wisdom. Help us to be busy with our hands, faithful with our time, and productive in our work.

Give us stamina for the day, helping us see that all the little things are not really little in Your economy. May we be encouraged in the trenches and know that "greater is He that is in me than he that is in the world".

When we are tired, give us rest; when we are irritable, give us grace; when we are grumpy give us gratitude; and when we are spent, carry us on from there.

Losing my life to save it...

It's a Full Time Job

It's little wonder why so many full-time mothers feel burned out. Motherhood was once looked upon and rightly understood as a job in which a woman was to invest herself wholly. It was a known fact that training the characters and intellect of children, creating a home full of comforts, and maintaining the duties of a household took nothing less than all of a woman's time and effort.

However, the influences of the feminist movement have effectively turned motherhood into a peripheral pursuit; something she is supposed to squeeze in around all her "important" work.

And even though many of us understand this deception, we still harbor those lingering thoughts that somehow we need to be doing more.

Dear mother, you need a renewed understanding of how grandiose your life work is, regardless of what the culture says. You need to remember that it is the very power of motherhood that causes Satan to quell and seek to destroy it.

What you do every day is evangelism; it is "caring for the least of these"; it is serving, even as our Lord gave us His example.

It is enough.

Biblical womanhood encompasses a vast ministry which can't begin to be measured by one woman in one lifetime. One wife and one mother, by God's grace and with a battle cry, "Not my will but Thine be done", will launch the power of the living God in her home, and that power multiples, intensifies, and generations upon generations stand on her shoulders, reaching ever heavenward, though laden with humanity, pressing on to the prize before them.

DAY 5

When Motherhood is Stressful

Being a wife and mother at home is *hard* . . . can I get a witness? I'll never pretend it's not. Some days seem to flow rather seamlessly into the next, and other days are full of those *"you've got to be kidding me"* moments.

You know the days . . .

You're changing the baby's poopy diaper when you hear glass shatter on the floor. You must run because you know the other children are barefooted. *"Get out of the kitchen everybody!"* while you go get the broom. The phone rings. You let it ring this time, but make a mental note to check the number and call back. Another child screams from downstairs—not a *"help, I'm dying"* scream, but a *"he took my baby"* scream, so you know it needs dealt with but has to wait in light of this glass emergency. "Here, can you finish sweeping?", you hand the broom to an older child.

The scream downstairs was actually, "*He threw my doll in the toilet*" scream, so you begin to fish. "*Where's the baby?*" You ask.

"*Oh, she's playing in her room*". Oh good . . . you can relax a bit and take care of business. Oh my word, the other baby's on the bed without a diaper! (You know what that means.)

You remember that the seven-year old needed help with her math problem, so you hurry to diaper the baby . . . the other baby, the one playing sweetly in her room? Well she was, except she decided to dress her baby doll . . . with all the clothes out of her dresser.

Maybe it's a bit of exaggeration, maybe not. But I didn't even mention the delicious meal you must prepare, the shower and sprucing up you'll do for your husband (c'mon ladies), the phone calls, the appointments, the music lessons . . .

Now that I think about it, it takes nerves of steel to do this job! Last night, sitting in our living room, I heard the faint sound of the 2-year old dragging the kitchen chair up to the counter to retrieve a cookie. My husband was completely unaware. Now this is not an insult to men . . . but God gave them a special ability to tune things out, I think. He asked her, "*Where did you get that cookie?*" And I said, "*You didn't hear her dragging the chair?*" He grinned and shook his head. I said, "*That's it . . . I have sensory overload. I hear everything, I see everything, I smell everything . . .*"

But I said all that to say this . . . *in the midst of the chaos that can be* LIFE, *we simply* MUST *nurture the relationships in our home.* How we relate to our children and our husbands is paramount! It is *so easy* to let the frustrations, the "overload" squelch our daily joy, but with a little concerted effort, *we can demonstrate to our families the peace of God that transcends understanding.*

Do what you have to do . . . deep breath, a walk outside—whatever you need to keep the right perspective, do it. Relationships are not built in the scheduled "family time" you lay aside; they're made in the small moments all throughout the day. How you answer each other, whether you stop to listen and look each other in the eyes, a tender touch on the back or face or arm, all those reassurances that tell them, *"I'm on your side, and I love being with you".*

Satan is roaming the earth, seeking whom he may devour. He would like nothing else than to destroy our families through the little subtle ways we can neglect our relationships. There's a song..."*It's a slow fade.*" Families don't crumble in a day. But *"greater is He that is in you than he that is in the world".*

A few of my simple stress busters:

- *Smile.* Whether you feel like it or not. Force yourself to wear a big smile for a few minutes and it will change your countenance and even how you're feeling inside.
- *Sing.* A silly song if you have to.
- *Tickle.* This works well especially if the children are grumpy too.
- *A funny video.* I have been known to look up our favorite comedians on youtube for a quick stress relief—we all gather around and laugh.
- *A walk.*

- *Prayer.* Pray specifically for those around you who are suffering. That will bring things back to perspective in a hurry.

Jesus had to get away and rest every now and then, from all the people pulling on him. But He went away so that He could return quickly, with a renewed vigor to serve.

Day 6

A Letter to Myself:
The Important Motherhood Secret

You have a highly specialized job as your children's mother; you get the privilege of transferring, teaching, imparting and eternally shaping the lives of the people that have been given to you for just that purpose. In one sense, this is remarkable news. In another, it's rather terrifying.

Terrifying because the transferring, teaching, imparting and eternally shaping is done primarily *through the life you live.*

They don't learn what you tell them you want them to learn; they learn to become *what you are. Being is the most important thing you'll do as a mother. Being what you want them to be, being the person you say loves Jesus, being generous to others, being a godly wife, being a kind woman, being genuine.*

Or not . . .

You can tell them they should "be kindly affectioned" and "prefer one another". But unless you are *being* kindly affectioned, preferring others over yourself, they will only learn to be a hypocrite.

You can tell them what a godly wife is supposed to be—the virtue, the tongue governed by kindness, the crown to her husband—but they'll mostly grow up to be the kind of wife you are *being*.

You can tell them about God's grace and forgiveness, how His mercy covers you because you can't always BE what you need to be, but unless you reflect that mercy and grace in the inhaling and exhaling of a day, they will not truly learn its depth.

And this being . . . it is constant, with no reprieve. Which is, in fact, the heart of the matter . . . that you are always transferring *who you are to your children and so it matters who you are—who you are becoming*, far more than it matters what you mean to teach them.

So the answer? You seek Him and pursue Him hard with a reckless abandon of all else. You love Him wholly, follow Him completely and make it your only desire in life to become more and more like Him. You study Him, chase Him until you find yourself becoming more like Him.

Then you will raise children who become what you wish for them to become.

Don't forget to run, sometimes,
barefoot in the grass.

Day 7

On Mother-Forgiveness

There are deeply stabbing lessons of motherhood . . .

This one hit me in a split second. *In one instance I refused the apology.* Not completely refused, but a *"I'm still very upset with you and you apologize for the same thing over and over and over, and I just want to see change instead of another apol—"*

Heart sank. . . . I was spouting the very words I hoped I would never hear my Father say. And I feel sure I will not.

Stopped mid-sentence, tears streaming down both our faces.

"No . . . I'm so sorry. I beg God to forgive ME *for the same things over and over and—by His grace—I will continue to forgive you over and over as long as I live."*

Relief broke across the face . . . relief that could only come after such a terrifying thought that Mother had "met her forgiveness quota."

Perhaps you are encouraged.

While your children are little, cultivate an attitude of sacrifice. Sacrifice your peace for their fun, your clean kitchen floor for their help cracking eggs, your quiet moment for their long retelling of a dream. . . . Prioritize your children above the other work you need to get done. They are the only part of your work that really matters.

Rachel Jankovic, *Loving the Little Years*

Day 8

Remember, in the Busiest Season

There is so much to be done, and yet what our children need from us is not hard. *Time, tenderness, instruction and direction.* They need to walk alongside us in life. That is how we impart to them what is important. That is how they come to trust us and believe us and allow us to transmit the great lessons of life. Do I let them into my life? Or do I shoo them away so I can get more done?

Does the pressing list of my day rob my children of a first-morning smile? Does my schedule squeeze out a mid-day hug? Can I let them into everything—the essence of building relationships, speaking through my actions—*"You are important to me right now"*?

Do they know they are valued, and that I like being with them? Do I converse with them, ask questions and then listen to the answers? Do I give them a chance to be who they are?

When motherhood feels too hard, drop the extra stuff, and focus on the few, important things. You are a tender of souls. You don't have to keep the house perfectly clean and you can even use paper plates sometimes. In the busiest season, love, laugh and relax.

The truth is that biblical motherhood doesn't mean we're promised postcard-perfect days where we lounge together with our little ones on the porch swing in white starched dresses sipping lemonade and singing in harmony. Homegrown children take a lot of hard work—and sometimes "it ain't pretty". Other times, it's breathtaking.

Jennie Chancey & Stacy McDonald,
Passionate Housewives, Desperate for God.

Day 9

5 Ways to Be a Better Mother

1. Take time to deal with strife in the home,
   refusing the urge to just "make it stop". Use
   Scripture to address harsh words and selfish
   attitudes. A few of my favorite:

   · "Pleasant words are a honeycomb, sweet
     to the soul and health to the bones."
   · "A soft answer turns away wrath, but a
     harsh word stirs up anger."
   · "Be kind one to another, with brotherly
     love, in honor, preferring one another."

2. Avoid distractions that hinder child training. If necessary, let the phone ring. Set strict
   parameters around your computer time. Say
   "no" to excessive outside activities. Be present,
   body and mind.
3. Taking a walk on a hard day will do wonders
   to clear your mind and help you gain needed
   perspective.

4. Put some space between incidents and your response to it. Use opportunities of failure to teach repentance and humility. Much worse than blowing it is the refusal to admit it and ask forgiveness.

5. Assess whether you have emphasized team work in the home, with everyone doing his share. If not, cheerfully reincorporate that into your daily training. It will make a huge difference in how smoothly things run. Can a child wash the lettuce? Collect the laundry? Set the table? Team work makes the day easier.

Life, learning, joy and growth. Those are the things we want to characterize our homes. Yes, we fall down. *But warriors get back up again.*

The daily tasks that make up the fabric of our lives are necessary and they help us weave into our children the proper ingredients for soul-growth, but we cannot "miss the forest for the trees", getting so preoccupied with daily routine, cleaning and organizing, that our children become just another task.

They are people . . . they are eternal . . . they are worth our lives.

Deliberate Moments of Motherhood

Mothers wear more hats than Minnie Pearl. A friend recently called and described the feeling of "wearing 10 hats while riding a unicycle". Yep, we're all nodding heads.

Which is why deliberate mothering is so important. Deliberate mothering involves, to me, those seemingly smaller things, that are actually the bigger things, that can get so easily crowded out in a busy day.

Things like lingering eye contact, both during instruction and to express deep fondness. Taking time to cuddle small children—and big ones, read to them or just enjoy child-talk.

Taking walks, talking of God's greatness, His provision for daily bread, His new morning-mercy, and His deep love for us—small moments of greatness.

Deliberate mothering is remembering to teach eager little hands how to crack an egg, and not get too upset when they drop it on the floor . . . because that moment holds an even bigger "deliberate opportunity". (I write it . . . but I'm still aspiring to live it.)

A word of friendship, a word of inspiration ("I love that part of who you are"), small moments each day that weave together a strong, beautiful tapestry of who our children will become.

I will interject a word of warning here: the opposite it also true. If the bulk of their days is spent receiving insult and injury, either by a parent or by peers who seem to default to "survival of the fittest", so much is lost and so much of that tapestry is left thread-bare.

Gigantic days are made up of small, deliberate moments. Let's make them.

Bring on the Hassle

Sometimes it's very hard, but more often, we let the pile of daily hassles make it hard, robbing us of our joy.

You know the hassles . . . car breakdowns, computer breakdowns, air conditioner break downs, the flu, traffic jams, bickering siblings, overflowing toilets—they can be managed, but if we don't keep the right perspective, we can really miss out on life!

> "For to you it has been granted for Christ's sake, not only to believe in Him but also to suffer for His sake." (Philippians 1:29)

It is when we get into the state of thinking that life is about escaping hardship, that the hardships become unbearable. *If I don't expect hardship and hassles in life, when they inevitably come, I will have the wrong response.*

Of course I'm not saying we should be looking for them, but rather understanding that they are as normal a part of life as the setting of the sun! If we change our frame of mind, then when the hassles of the day start to pile up, we don't throw our hands up in "unfair despair". We cope, we deal, because this is life and we are prepared.

I think of this every time I hear someone say "she shouldn't have anymore children because she mentioned one day how tired she was." Motherhood is just like any other work—tiring and hard. Is that a reason to quit?

My Dad is a farmer/construction worker. Life on the farm is such a great place to see this principle. It's 98 degrees, there are hundreds of hay bales on the ground, it's threatening rain and he's hired a small crew to help. Then the baler breaks down— happens every summer, usually several times. He is as cool-headed as they come. Always. Why? Because life happens. He doesn't curse and spit and ask "*Why?!*" He just handles the situation with perfect perspective. He usually loses time and money, but in the big picture, it's only time and money.

When my hassles come, I stand to lose more than what the hassle brings. . . . I may lose time, money, energy, yes—but if I have the wrong perspective, I lose the chance to teach those around me a deeper lesson. I lose the chance to allow God to mold me into His image. I lose the chance to teach my children how to handle their hassles.

I want to be more like my Dad . . . like Christ . . . when the crowd presses in, and the heat bears down, and the pressures rise. Life has its hassles, but in all things, we are more than conquerors through Christ. *Bring the hassles on* . . . each one is an opportunity—a test—waiting to happen.

Day 12

Endurance

Motherhood is really, at its core, about perseverance and deliberate, focused endurance.

I don't mean just the physical kind...more often, it is the emotional and spiritual kind. It requires the kind of tenacity that frankly, few women in our age are willing to develop.

Not the tenacity to simply run a household, though the mechanics of that are a very real part of our job. *But the "motherhood" I'm talking about encompasses a whole world besides; a world where hearts are painstakingly drawn out, attitudes are carefully monitored and molded, and life-lessons that can only be taught through the zeal of a mother are learned.*

Quite frankly, we've probably all had days we thought, "this would be easier if someone else were doing it". And someone else might be able to handle those mechanics I mentioned.

But we're talking about mother-love—that all-encompassing vocation that has been given only to us.

I get tired. I'm tired now, which is what prompted me to write this. I get grouchy, and start to look around and only see too many pairs of shoes out of place, dust under the couch, trash that could so easily be placed in the can left on the table until I point it out.

Painstaking.

But I *must* reboot, and remind myself that the mechanics—that is, how I handle the mechanics, are intricately tied to this bigger thing that we do... this growing of souls, and launching of good, sturdy men and women.

I cannot allow myself to be too tired for too long. Grace is given, yes, but then I must draw, not from my own strength, but from that source of never-ending power that comes from the One who has called me to this.

I have to think before I speak...the pile of shoes may be bothersome, but they also may be an opportunity to shape my character which will transfer to my children.

The moment of bickering calls me to dig deep into the well of my being and carves out of me a more patient and loving spirit—if I let it. That, too, is simultaneously working in my children's character.

This short time is fleeting...they will carry a part of me into the rest of their lives. Which part?

Get alone, get quiet, get still. And ask the Lord to bring the vision back, if you are struggling to hold on to it. *This is big...rise to the occasion on the wings of Him Who is able.*

Not Alone

Kelly Crawford

Though now I stand in a valley dark,
I do not stand alone,
There is One who stands with me,
so gentle yet so strong.
He is my refuge and my shield,
He holds me in His arms—
He's my Heavenly Father
and in Him I'm safe from harm.
He never promised me a life
that's free from pain or tears,
But promised He would never leave
and that allays my fears.
Because no matter what I face
or how my heart may break,
My Father knows and hurts with me,
He longs to soothe the ache.
I know not what tomorrow holds
and yesterday is gone,
So on my knees I pray today

for strength to carry on.
Father grant me faith and hope
as I walk through the storm,
And may I reach the other side
stronger than before.

Of Suffering and New Beginnings

Don't we all inhale the newness of an approaching year, saying "this year will be different, better—I will be different, better." We write lists, make charts, set goals—all of which we should. And then the sneaking memory of our failures from the year before creeps in and tells us "don't bother".

We strive—and there is place for striving—but mostly we forget "The Lord will go before you." We strive and fail, so we make more charts, try harder and finally give up...*unless*, at the end of our striving we realize *"His grace is sufficient for me; for when I am weak, then He is strong"*.

Do I ever just leave the room, go to a quiet place, fall on my knees and strive there? What would life be like if I made a habit of this striving?

"He is close to the broken and contrite."

I am the manager of my home, and as such, there *are* lists to make, things to improve—practical areas to govern.

But as the year begins, I will purpose to wrap these duties in humble prayer and petition to the Father.

"If God is for us, who can be against us?"

And then, like the demonstration of placing larger rocks in the jar first so the smaller ones fit around it, I will prioritize the day, and put the big stuff in first. The stuff of eternal weight, no matter what others say is the most important.

I am prone to think that motherhood is a lot of crying out to God to bear me up, and a lot of smiling, talking and learning to enjoy my children as I try to show them glimpses of a Savior. Can I do those things? Won't everything else fit in around that?

What is your wilderness? More importantly, what is it wringing out of your heart? A shaking fist, or the cry..." *Though He slay me, yet will I trust Him*"?

Look past your present suffering. Thank God for the crucible that will melt away the dross.

"Refine me Lord, so I may be more like You."

DAY 15

So Much Living

Side by side, living life, talking, sharing, smiling at each other. Just being here with them . . . I'm thankful in a thousand ways.

And even when we're not smiling . . . when tempers flare and we say the things we shouldn't. Praise God for days that don't go well! Praise Him for the thousands of chances we have to live forgiveness! To show them that messing up doesn't mean losing favor . . . that forgiveness is there again and again. No, I don't like it either at the time but it knits the gospel into our hearts, makes us humble and reminds us of our constant need of a Savior.

What could be more important? So many lessons to learn in the ordinary.

So much living to do in a day.

Oh that God would give every mother a vision of the glory and splendor of the work that is given to her when a babe is place in her bosom to be nursed and trained! Could she have but one glimpse in to the future of that life as it reaches on into eternity; could she look into its soul to see its possibilities; could she be made to understand her own personal responsibility for the training of this child, for the development of its life, and for its destiny,—she would see that in all God's world there is no other work so noble and so worthy of her best powers, and she would commit to no others hands the sacred and holy trust given to her.

J.R. Miller

DAY 16

Of Planting, Dying and Living

"...unless a kernel of wheat falls to the ground and dies, it remains only a single seed. But if it dies, it produces many seeds. The man who loves his life will lose it, while the man who hates his life in this world will keep it for eternal life. Whoever serves me must follow me; and where I am, my servant also will be. My Father will honor the one who serves me." (John 12:23–26)

These impossible words from our Lord...impossible, that is, for one who does not possess the spirit of the living God.

And still so hard for the one who does.

This verse made me think of motherhood and children. "Unless a kernel of wheat falls to the ground and dies..."

There is a dying to produce life. God knew that. And that death that seems painful to us at times, He knew would bring about "many seeds".

I thought about "many seeds". And "olive shoots around your table". And fruitfulness. *When we "die" to our fear, our control, our plans, our pride—when we die to ourselves, we become able to increase with so much more capacity.* Both in sheer number, and in our ability to become a true disciple of Christ. (*"Nevertheless it is not I, but He that lives in me."*)

No, our culture doesn't esteem motherhood, because it's not very fond of dying. It doesn't esteem the things of God for that same reason.

But those who have tasted of that wonderful gift of grace know about the secret—the underground miracle of rebirth and producing many seeds.

As mothers, can we cling to this analogy, glory in our "many seeds", and long for nothing more than to allow God the room to do with us what He wills?

If not, He'll keep us dying all the time, until we finally do give up and die once and for all...for His glory and purpose.

Motherhood is no profession for those who want results *now*. It's not the place for those without long-term vision and the tenacity with which to carry out that vision. It's not for the weak-kneed or faint. If ever we need mothers willing to plant the seeds for the next generation it is now.

Planting is hard work; if you had a garden this year, think back over your labors. The heat, the bugs, the weeds, the back-breaking work...it's a job that one must tend consistently and without fruit for a while.

But oh the harvest!

A story was told of an old, beautiful church. After hundreds of years, the beams began to rot. As the elders discussed the remedy, the oldest member motioned them to come to the back. He pointed across the field behind the church where grew some of the largest, most impressive oak trees the eyes have ever seen.

"When the founders of this church built it, they knew that in time, long after they were gone, the beams would need to be replaced, and could not be replaced with just anything. So they planted those trees there for that purpose."

Now that's vision!

We've got to plant the seeds of cedars (or oaks!) that we will never even see! Not only are we called to pass on a spiritual legacy to our children, but the Bible speaks of our children's children. We must raise our children in such a way that their faith grows roots far into the next generation.

It takes deliberate life-work to do that! No, it isn't done apart from God's grace and divine order. But it also isn't done by a flippant attitude that takes advantage of that grace. We must speak of Him, live for Him, be willing to die for Him and pass that fervent love on to our children.

We want results now...we want fruit now...we want instant trees. But God has never worked like that. Sometimes His purposes through someone or some group of people can't even be realized until long after they're gone. That's why faith in the unseen is *so* important to Christians!

Will members of the next generation be able to see the diligence of the "planters" in this one?

We cannot be weary in well-doing! There's a forest depending on our faithfulness. The seeds we plant should bear fruit for generation after generation.

Only He can see the big picture; we need only trust His sovereignty and keep planting, hoeing and cultivating our trees!

Don't forget to use your crock pot! Find some great recipes, throw all the ingredients in a gallon zip-lock bag and freeze. You'll have ready meals for your family and for unexpected needs around you.

DAY 17

The Glamor of Washing Feet

Washing feet. Not a glamorous job. But a job worthy of the King of Kings to perform with love and humility.

But there's more. He then admonishes us to be like Him. "Oh Lord, I want to be like you...I really do", we say. He replies, "then wash their feet".

"No, I mean I want an honorable ministry....ya know, one that other people will point to and say, 'my, how godly she is!'. " And Jesus says, "then you have shall have no part with me".

It's no accident that everything the Lord requires of us is hatefully opposed to our nature. "Love your enemies....be last...lose your life...crucify the flesh... and yes, wash feet." But the beautiful irony is that only when we submit to living a life that He asks of us, does His grace gush in like a tidal wave, and carry us up on its crest, enabling us to do the hardest of things.

We are proud, stubborn creatures, who, if we find ourselves forced to "wash feet" for any length of time, begin, before we're even done, to throw ourselves a pity party, and evoke the sympathies of others to soothe our poor, pathetic lots in life. But the Lord says "wash feet", and do it cheerfully.

Why??? Because it conforms us to His image. Because it's not the glory we receive here that counts for anything...it's the eternal reward of faithful, consistent, often unnoticed obedience.

Motherhood provides one of the greatest opportunities to "wash feet" that I can think of. And isn't it just like the Lord to give us a job that often seems too big to handle? "I can't handle anymore children". Of course you can't. That's the whole point! He *knows* you can't, but He is begging you to let Him show his power through you!

Already this morning I have cleaned up two full bowls of spilled milk (one all over the cloth cushion of the kitchen chair), settled I don't know how many disputes, had to discern why the little ones are fussing, when to discipline, when to gently listen, urge the children to "speak gently", meanwhile pushing down my urge to explode while mopping the floor, answering math questions, changing diapers, picking up the living room . . . again, washing dishes . . . well, you know . . . your list is as long as mine!

And for some reason, today seems harder than most. I had already planned to "tell my husband all about it" when he called. As if that would be a blessing to him, or to my listening children!

So the Lord beckons me to take a deep breath, retreat into a quiet place, and pour out to Him my frustrations.

Then, pick up a clean towel, smile, and go wash some more feet!

Washing Feet

Kelly Crawford

A mother toiled with all her might
Tending needs both day and night.
Cleaning, laundry, dirty dishes,
Changing diapers, giving kisses.
No one saw her faithful deeds
The sacrifice for others' needs.
She never got a company raise
Or heard the applause of worldly praise.
But still she labored diligently
She knew what others couldn't see.
And then one night a dream told true
About that treasure this mother knew.
She dreamt of seeing her Savior's face
And then she felt His strong embrace.
Before she had time to even speak
The King of Kings knelt at her feet.
A water basin soon appeared
She gasped in horror through her tears.
She begged of Him to take her seat

To let her wash her Savior's feet.
He just smiled and said with ease
"You did, when you served the least of these."

Are Your Prayers Hindered?

I needed help. I gathered up what strength I had and knelt to pray: *"Lord, I can't do this...I need you to help me."*

It wasn't necessarily the wrong prayer. But it was the wrong motive. I wanted a quick help, quick answers to my frustrations, quick relief for my pain. We are bound up by time and space, so short-sighted and therefore prone to pray with wrong motives.

The Lord cared about my hard day, yes. But not nearly as much as He cared about the fact that I had unconfessed sin, an unrepentant heart and therefore broken fellowship with my Father. Often, just like a burn isn't pleasant to the hand but is ultimately a mild, helpful consequence, so our pain is meant to bring our attention to impending danger to our souls. It is meant to stop us, force us to reckon with the Savior until we are right again.

Are you wrestling in your spirit? Is there unrest in your soul? Perhaps the pain is that of a loving Father, desperately begging your presence with Him, your repentance, so that the sweetness of fellowship might be restored.

Listen, search your heart and humble yourself in the sight of Him who wants to restore the joy of your salvation.

My Spaghetti-Smeared Generation

Farmer holds a few ordinary seeds in his hand.

But he doesn't see seeds. He also doesn't see, or rather, doesn't *dwell* on the work he's about to give himself to.

Okay, he does see the seeds, and dirt, and sweat and weeds. But it's what lies beyond the seeing . . . it's the *vision.*

He really sees a swelling harvest from that handful of humble seeds—a miracle he really can't fully understand.

He sees results of his labor and the fruit of his hands and the many who will be blessed by it for years to come.

Because next year, his seeds will yield more seeds.

And some days he'll be scratching in the dirt and sweating and seeing nothing but weeds. But he knows what's underneath if he'll only persevere, and he has the *faith* required to believe it will burst forth from the ground.

Someone asked me how I could be excited about a ninth baby.

"Because I don't see a baby".

Well, yes I do, and he/she is magnificently more wonderful than a handful of seeds!

But I see more than a baby.

I see a harvest . . . the fruit of our love, the physical reminder of "two becomes one", the labor of our hands through the years, a heritage, for me, from my Father.

My vision goes beyond that sweet little face and all the messes I know I will clean up, and the midnight feedings that aren't easy, the squabbles and the stains on the furniture, the tears and laughter, and the days I just want quiet. . . .

There's a whole generation underneath that spaghetti-smeared face that's been given to me.

And it's worth it.

And I want to be here when the harvest is fully ripe. . . . .

But I won't.

Because the seeds we plant now will grow beyond us and the harvest will become unable to be measured.

So I will keep pulling the weeds, planting the seeds, nurturing, watering, tending and praying for growth, thanking God for the miracles.

And I will have the *faith* to believe that His glory will burst forth.

When we understand that our whole existence is to glorify the Lord, we live each moment differently. We get about our Father's business. We don't measure "if we should have children" by their convenience or how many vacations it will cost me or whether I can pursue my favorite pastime or career. We don't have children to look cute in their ball uniforms and homemade hair bows.

We fall down on our knees with the grave responsibility of stewardship over these children, these people who will either further the Kingdom or be a blight on society, based largely on our diligence to the duty of raising them.

Day 21

Overwhelmed

I am asked quite often for advice on mothering lots of little ones. Truly a young mother with several little ones is in the thick of it. Keeping perspective is the number one important thing. This season is temporary. Some of the things that drive you crazy about it now you will miss later. Try to savor these days.

Practically speaking, what can a mother do to maximize her time? I think it's important to understand that not one of us has an identical situation or is in the exact same season of life, and not one of us has it all together. We can learn from each other, but it's fruitless to copy. We need to begin with the prayer and pursuit of maximizing our time based on *our* specific circumstances and adjust our expectations accordingly. We need to avoid comparing (though we all do it, don't we?)

- *Multi-task.* Most mothers are natural at this anyway, but sometimes a deliberate effort can "multiply" your time. For example, I may ask a child to narrate his reading to me while I wash dishes or hang up clothes in my room. I have found that stretching/exercising is a great thing to bring the little ones around for—it doubles for focused time with them, maybe while the older ones are doing their chores. Sometimes we practice math facts while running errands. I always try to do a chore if I'm talking on the phone too.

- *Pare down the schedule.* For us, this is a biggie. Often when people ask me, "how do you find time for A,B or C", it becomes easier to understand when they find out we don't have a lot of extra-curricular activities. We are blessed to have our music teacher come to our home, as well as our art teacher, which are our only "extra" things. We spend very little time driving around to this or that which allows for a lot of time for other pursuits.

- *No TV.* We watch movies on selected days of the week, but we don't have the temptation of watching regular programming because we don't have it. It would be a huge weakness for all of us if we did (we discover that on vacations), so we did away with it a long time ago. You'd be amazed at what can be accomplished without it!

- *Delegating responsibilities.* Don't underestimate what your children can do, and don't rob them of the opportunity to do it! I heard of one mom who made the bottom drawer the silverware drawer. Her four-year-old was in charge of putting it away and setting the table with it. She felt so big to have her own job and it was one less thing for Mom. As a general rule: don't do what a younger child can do. Also, it's more efficient in the long run to take a little extra time now to train a child how to do a job properly. You are the manager; that doesn't mean you do all the work.

· *Maintain realistic expectations.* I had a relative who pulled all her furniture and all her kitchen appliances out and cleaned underneath them once a week-the stove, the refrigerator, everything. That's taking the house cleaning thing a bit too far, in my opinion, and will most likely absorb time that could be better spent elsewhere. A tidy home is good, but obsession is a problem. Choose a few times in the day where everyone tidies up and try not to stress about messes in between. Lay down some basic rules: put one group of toys away before you play with another, take your plate to the sink after meals, pick up your room before bedtime, or whatever rules work for your home. And then relax and enjoy this season with little ones, knowing one day you really will miss the Play-Doh smashed into the carpet.

· *Define areas of stress and seek to change them.* Noise is a big stress to me, but we have nine children; what's a mom to do? We continuously work on "inside voices" and calm play. This doesn't mean they can't laugh and have fun, but they understand there's a difference between inside and outside. I've been around children who were just in the habit of yelling, screaming and running inside (and of course they carried that habit into other public places) and such behavior is only the fault of the parent who allows it. Moderation should be taught early and includes a reasonable expectation that our children know the difference in inside and outside volumes and are able to exhibit self-control. It should simply be taught as an expression of "loving your neighbor".

Some moms get their time sucked up by chatty (but dear) friends during school hours. An older mother once told me that she absolutely didn't answer the phone before noon, and that doing so made all the difference in her home.

Some moms find meals an especially difficult time. What are some ways you could prepare ahead to make this an easier part of the day? (Have one cooking day for the whole week? Simplify your meals for this season? Barter meals with a friend for something else?) When our dish washer was broken we mostly used paper plates at my husband's insistence that it was worth it. Whatever works!

Identify the areas in your home that cause the most stress and ask your husband to help you find a solution.

These are just a few of the ideas I gathered from my own experience. Think through your life carefully and see how many solutions you can find!

At the end of the year we turn with eagerness to all that God has for the future, and yet anxiety is apt to arise from remembering the yesterdays. Our present enjoyment of God's grace is apt to be checked by the memory of yesterday's sins and blunders. But God is the God of our yesterdays, and He allows the memory of them in order to turn the past into a ministry of spiritual culture for the future. God reminds us of the past lest we get into a shallow security in the present.

Oswald Chambers

Mother, Take the Time

Kelly Crawford

I used to race, I used to hurry,
I used to fret and frown and worry.
My children thought they had new names—
"Hurry Up" and "We're Gonna Be Late"!
Even when we were at home—
Laundry, cleaning, answer the phone . . .
I never had the extra time
to sit and cherish these children of mine.
But in His grace the Lord broke through
And I saw everything anew.
We have but only a few days here,
to love and share and pull them near.
And while there're things that must be done,
Our lives are like the setting sun.
While its light is burning bright,
Before we face, alone, the night,
Let's stop the madness of this race—
Let's take back a slower pace!
Look into those grinning faces,

Plan your day with lots of spaces.
Grab a hand and take a walk,
Listen while your children talk.
Let them show you childhood things,
Take turns laughing on the swing.
Snuggle up beside the fire,
Kiss the hurt left by a brier.
Meet them with a morning smile,
Go out and fish a little while.
Choose carefully how you spend your time.
Don't wait until you suddenly find
The wrenching grief of a heart that aches
Who loved too little and found out too late.

The Mission Field of Children

I realized a truth years ago that profoundly changed my ability to cope with the hard things of motherhood.

Expectations are paramount in dealing with life issues. They either better prepare us, or ill-prepare us for our circumstances. And expectations, both from ourselves and others, change everything we view about motherhood.

I was reading a missionary letter we received from some friends overseas. They described the grave living conditions—of no indoor plumbing, rampant disease, overwhelming heat and brewing tribal unrest in the bush where they were ministers. Several ironies struck me that day.

First, despite the hardships they faced, they were propelled by a force—the force of love they felt for these people as they were determined, no matter what, to share the gospel with them.

Secondly, no one questioned their plight. It was expected hardship—that was the life of an overseas missionary. No one "tsked" them for choosing a hard life, but admired their bravery in being willing to face whatever came as the natural result of their missionary calling.

The parallel to motherhood was astounding. If I had the same propelling force as one "called to missions", would I brave my minor difficulties with more fortitude? *I am precisely called to missions, to bring my children, and anyone else in my path, to the living knowledge and truth of the gospel. What then can come to sway that mission?*

When Paul was persecuted for preaching the gospel—that force that propelled him—he didn't measure his "success" by his difficulties. He didn't wring his hands over "what God's will is" because he had such hard days, yes, "unproductive" days. *He was called.* There was no turning back, even as he must have cried out for God's sustaining grace. He set his face like flint and charged ahead, through joys and perils.

As did our Lord and every other saint of God that has ever been called to the life-changing mission of making disciples.

Mothers are no different. Our difficulties should not come as surprise but as a badge of honor, a "sharing in the sufferings of our Lord" and others who love Him. Press on, dear one, in your missionary calling.

Crying From the Depths[1]

Whatever condition or situation in which we find ourselves, however much our hearts are broken, our expectations crushed under the weight of affliction, we must never cease calling upon the Lord. All our help and hope in such times lies in making our plea to our Father, waiting upon him, and trusting his promises. Though in frustration our first tendency is to rush to find a solution, any solution, or run away and hide, or seek forgetfulness through distraction and vanity, trouble has not come upon us accidentally. It has come from the hand of the Lord for this very purpose: that utterly emptied of ourselves and having the multitude of idols in our hearts smashed, we might learn that he is our rock and fortress.

You may have never felt the need to cry like Jonah from the belly of the fish, or Daniel threatened

---

1 Chris Strevel, "Crying From the Depths", http://www.covenant-rpcus.org/articles/from-the-pastors-desk/crying-from-the-depths, accessed 11-3-12

by Darius, or David hounded by Saul. None of us
will ever find himself in the garden with our Lord,
so suffering under the sorrows of death that angelic
assistance was required to preserve and strengthen
him. You may think your troubles quite small in
comparison, unworthy of such ardent crying to the
Lord, or that you had better just bear them the best
you can.

*But have you considered that though the Lord may not have
called you to walk in the darkest places, you have no less need
to call upon him? Our trials, as our gifts and responsibilities,
are not to be measured by those of others, for God makes men
to differ (1 Cor. 4:7).* We are exactly the same, however,
in our need to call upon the Lord. Our trials would
be more sanctified to our good, less embittering,
if we would but learn this one simple lesson: small
or great, the Lord wants us to call upon him at all
times, especially in our hour of need."

Each new morning dawns with the clouds of guilt
and sorrow engulfing you with an impenetrable gray
veil. You think of your many faults as a parent or a
spouse; your house seems more like a mirror of your
failings than a home in which to rest. What are you
to do? Psalm 130 comes to mind. "Out of the depths
have I cried unto thee, O Lord."

Thus, when we ask him to "hear our voice and
be attentive to our supplications" (Ps. 130:2), this
must be nothing else but a bringing forward of Jesus
Christ, the Father's Beloved and Anointed: his
merits, not ours, his wisdom, not ours, his good-
ness, worthiness, and blood gains the ear of the
God of the universe, not our efforts, grief, or tears.
We are heard when we bring forward his name in

faith, cling to his cross, and trust his advocacy at the Father's right hand.

We must turn, then, from thoughts of self-worth, as well as from our demerits, for the former does not admit us or the latter exclude us. His ear and heart are open to us because his ear and heart are open to his Son. Through him, we are freely invited to cry out to him from the depths. "...our plea becomes not so much for our circumstances to be changed, sin to be overcome, health to be recovered, a longed-for blessing to be obtained—though he often grants these after we have been buried in the belly of the fish—but praise to him for his constancy, for the hidden manna of his promises, whose sustaining power is felt only after we have been humbled and emptied of self in the desert.

DAY 25

And the Joy Dawns[2]

Joy begins to dawn, even in woe, for "in his presence is fullness of joy" (Ps. 16:11). At the very least, even if more weeping in the night looms before us, hope arises in our hearts, for God is hope: that none of these troubles are outside his control but are rather brought by his hand to humble and teach us, to make us more dependent upon him and trusting of his promises, and to empty us of our vanity that we might be filled with his purity and peace through the indwelling Spirit."

But the chief benefit of crying to the Lord will be received only if we wait patiently for him and hope in his word. We do not like to wait; the pain is too deep, the struggle too wearying. The Lord will not relieve the pressure until you know that he is your portion, that the inestimable blessing of crying to him is to find him as your all, your very life.

---

2   Chris Strevel, "Crying from the Depths", http://www.covenant-rpcus.org/articles/from-the-pastors-desk/crying-from-the-depths, accessed 11-3-12

How else will we ever truly forsake the world and devote ourselves to seeking first his kingdom and righteousness unless our vain delusions and worldliness begin to be purged away in the furnace of affliction?

The depths, the floods of life, all the Lord's waves and billows rolling over us, have one main purpose—to drive us back to his word.

The Lord will bring all his children into the depths. Some of us are so weak that he only causes us to walk through the shallows. He drags some of us further out into the choppy sea. His purpose is the same. There is nothing but sinking, shifting sand in us. He causes the winds to howl and raises a storm surge. We thought we were safe in the little boat of our life. We row with all our might to shore, any shore, to get out of the way of the storm. But these storms are from him and cannot be avoided, not only because it is impossible to escape from his will but also because in the midst of the storm, even if we seem to be thrown overboard and are flailing in the depths, he will teach us that we are his beloved, preserved children.

His promises are enough for us. His mercy is sure. He will have us cry to him. He sits as King above the flood not simply in immoveable, glorious sovereignty but also to cover us with his wings and teach us that we are secure, forgiven, and blessed in him. Cry to him from the depths, dear believer. It is unlikely the wind will immediately subside, but if you will cling to his promises and hope in his mercy, you will find the Lord of Hosts, your Father in

Jesus, a calm in the eye of the storm and light when all other lights go out.

The Kingdom Choice of Raising Children

"The efforts which a mother makes for the improvement of her child in knowledge and virtue, are necessarily retired and unobtrusive. The world knows nothing of them; and hence the world has been slow to perceive how powerful and extensive is this secret and silent influence. . . . the influence which is exerted upon the mind during the first eight or ten years of existence, in a great degree guides the destinies of that mind for time and eternity! And as the mother is the guardian and guide of the early years of life, from her goes the most powerful influence in the formation of the character of man." — *John Abbott*

When Christians stop being "Kingdom-minded", they stop making Kingdom choices. Choices like devoting a life to raising the next generation to love God, to honor authority and to live wisely. The very church of Christ has so degraded the blessing of children (and thus minimized a mother's work), that it is almost unthinkably ignorant. For how can we expect to pass to our children, the torch of passion and faithfulness to our Savior, unless we have made it our chiefest aim to daily impress His character onto their hearts?

When we understand that our whole existence is to glorify the Lord, we live each moment differently. *We get about our Father's business.* We don't measure "if we should have children" by their convenience or how many vacations it will cost me or whether I can pursue my favorite pastime or career. We don't have children to look cute in their ball uniforms and homemade hair bows.

We fall down on our knees with the grave responsibility of stewardship over these children, these people who will either further the Kingdom or be a blight on society, based largely on our diligence to the duty of raising them.

Mothers, you must govern your home well. It is the cruelest act of motherhood that you should neglect to teach your children to obey the loving authority over them. For in doing so, you make them unable to submit to God.

Children who have not learned self-government stand to be the most wretched of all men and women, loathing you for your indulgences.

But don't you see, it isn't harsh! It wells up from the deepest love, the deepest desire to see our children walking in truth and evokes sheer delight to walk beside them.

When I see my children through Kingdom-eyes, their vices aren't irritations that bug me and cause me to be angry; they are offenses that sober me and call me to the tireless and tender action of praying for, teaching and tending the garden of their souls.

My children are the very happiest when I have loved them enough to require gratitude, obedience and honor. Their little faces light up into mine when they sense my tenderest sincerity toward their character.

And then, to place my hands on their heads, kneel over them and pray . . .

> "Father, you have blessed me with this child. Thank you that she is growing to love You, thank you that she is obedient, and I pray that she will serve you all the days of her life" . . .

causes a heart-smile to break across their faces, and they know—it sinks down deep and they *know* that I am in this for life, through tears, joys and hardship. I am their advocate, and I will stop short of nothing to give "my life for yours" in these few years they are mine.

Happiness in This Life[3]

Margaret had a sudden tender memory of the days when Theodore and Duncan and Rob were all babies in turn. Her mother would gather the little daily supply of fresh clothes from bureau and chest every morning, and carry the little bath-tub into the sunny nursery window, and sit there with only a bobbing downy head and waving pink fingers visible from the great warm bundle of bath apron. . . .

And she had sometimes wished, or half formed the wish, that she and Bruce had been the only ones—! Yes, came the sudden thought, but it wouldn't have been Bruce and Margaret, after all, it would have been Bruce and Charlie.

Good God! That was what women did, then, when they denied the right of life to the distant, unwanted, possible little person! Calmly, constantly, in all placid philosophy and self-justification, they kept from the world—not only the troublesome new baby, with his tears and his illnesses, his merciless

---

3   Taken from *Mother,* by Kathleen Norris

exactions, his endless claim on mind and body and spirit—but perhaps the glowing beauty of a Rebecca, the buoyant indomitable spirit of a Ted, the sturdy charm of a small Robert, whose grip on life, whose energy and ambition were as strong as Margaret's own!

Margaret stirred uneasily, frowned in the dark. It seemed perfectly incredible, it seemed perfectly impossible that if Mother had had only the two—and how many thousands of women didn't have that!—she, Margaret, a pronounced and separate entity, traveled, ambitious, and to be the wife of one of the world's great men, might not have been lying here in the summer night, rich in love and youth and beauty and her dreams!

It was all puzzling, all too big for her to understand. But she could do what Mother did, just take the nearest duty and fulfill it, and sleep well, and rise joyfully to fresh effort.

Oh that God would give every mother a vision of the glory and splendor of the work that is given to her when a baby is placed in her bosom to be nursed and trained! Could she have but one glimpse into the future of that life as it reaches on into eternity; could she look into its soul to see its possibilities; could she be made to understand her own personal responsibility for the training of this child, for the development of its life, and for its destiny,—she would see that in all God's world there is no other work so noble and so worthy of her best powers, and she would commit to no other hands the sacred and holy trust given to her.

J.R. Miller

Fingerprints All Over Them

Is it hard sometimes? Sure it is...like all things that are worth anything in life. Being a full time wife and mom to six children is challenging, especially as my pregnant belly begins to impair me and make my feet swell if I'm up too much.

And I fail. Sometimes, miserably. I get impatient, I lose my temper, I scold for accidents, when a forgiving glance is in order.

The dishes are often piled up on the cabinet. The floor *always* needs to be mopped. I get my priorities upside down. Children disobey, forget, and we start all over again tomorrow.

But then a brown-skinned little girl with an angelic expression asks me, "Mommy, can I sit on your wap?" Or my oldest daughter tells me to sit down while she cleans up from supper...or I just watch the excitement on my son's face as he discovers a new "creature"...or the baby points intently at a book and babbles in quiet up and down tones, knowing exactly what she is saying.

I feel the soft punches of a new life inside me. She's a brand new thought of God, and she's the heartbeat of the love between my husband and me...

How can this not be the greatest life? The glorious opportunity to see them and be with them, and read to them, and laugh with them, and love with them, and learn with them—every minute of the day?!!!

Motherhood! To know these little people are going to grow up into men and women, and God has given me a small span of time to press my fingerprints all over them!

When I'm away from them only a short time, my arms ache to hold them, my fingers long to caress their soft faces. This is God's blessed gift...this is the abundant life.

Some days are hard. Some days are blissful. Some days are exhausting and you need to run to the Father and beg for more grace, more strength and a fresh perspective. Jesus was a discipler of souls. They pulled Him, tugged Him, pressed in around Him and took from Him at every turn. But he never lost sight of how precious they were, and how important His job of pointing to the Father, for the sake of their souls, was. He stole away to His quiet place, not to "find Himself", but to be renewed so He could go back and pour Himself out again.

Housework Again?

"I've swept the floor three times already and it's dirty again!"

Does this reality discourage you, make you want to walk away some days?

One of the reasons I believe many women shirk the duties of a full-time homemaker is that the idea of "doing the same mundane tasks" all day seems like drudgery. And it can be without the keen understanding of what is actually happening in our homes each day, and the powerful message we have the opportunity to preach "by the works of our hands".

> "... we *need* to understand the glory in the repetition; the glory that He is bringing about in us—in our families, when we gladly tend, gladly do it all over again!"

Most women are bothered by a disorderly home and lately I'm learning what an important trait this is in my life. Being bothered by it keeps me working at it. Created in His image, we, like Him, crave order. (The first task given to a human was to "tend the garden"—to keep order.) And after the Fall, the world set about decaying and losing order.

As image-bearers of our Creator, we were put here to daily restore order, on a small scale, in our small spaces, as a reflection of the One who is about restoring us, making order of the chaos through the continual renewing of His people. And if we aren't keeping order in our small space, decay is inevitable. Is it any wonder, then, why Satan is constantly about the business of removing the "order-keeper" from the home and/or distracting us from this "less-than-exciting" work?

As managers of our homes, we are given the task, the privilege, to "tend the garden". Weeds grow in gardens and they come back continually. Clean floors get dirty again, windows only shine for a little while and children need bathed over and over. And the physical order-keeping is only the beginning... tending the people there—the constant training of habits and character—is immensely large, causing us both to rejoice and to shudder at the job at hand.

But we *need* to understand the glory in the repetition; the glory that He is bringing about in us—in our families, when we gladly tend, gladly do it all over again!

A busy mom's home is not pristine; it need not be nor can it be where it is lived in ("Where no oxen are, the crib is clean . . ."); but there must be a continual work toward order, toward restoring what is in a constant state of decay. And this constant work is the way it should be. Don't be discouraged believing that the mundane is unimportant rather than embracing the privilege of being the one to whom it has been given to assist our God in restoring beauty, harmony and life into our homes, like He is doing in us.

And as we work about the day, we get to speak about this wonderful analogy to our children, to point to Him and to flesh out this lesson through every task.

As we work toward this order and find better ways to achieve it—the simple things like putting supper in the crock pot in the morning so that the transition to dinner time is smoother—our homes begin to reflect a sweetness that influence the people in it and the people that come by it.

It's a "working out", if you will, the order permeating *us,* and that work of restoration in the physical enables us to better glorify Him in all other realms of life.

It's not just picking up Legos for the hundredth time . . . it's Kingdom work, doing our part to make lovely and useful what would otherwise be decay and stagnant.

Wife & Mother:
Power to Grow or Destroy

"Lord, I want to be a wife who causes her husband to flourish, and a mother who causes her children to grow."

This was my earnest prayer after weeks of battling some emotional issues that have strained our family. If you are a wife and mother, I have good news and bad news: but it is the same news. You profoundly affect the atmosphere of your home. There is no way around it.

My emotional, spiritual and physical response to daily life can snowball to the rest of my family and bring peace and life or bring stress and destruction.

So when I prayed that prayer, I cried it from the depths of my soul. I have been brought to a place that is the end of myself. *"Nothing in my hands I bring, simply to thy cross I cling"* has become the song of my soul.

But the very good news is that the God of all our needs *is* sufficient. But He's waiting for us to realize there is no power in ourselves. He's waiting for us to "draw near to Him" so He can draw near to us.

There is a tidal wave of peace when we finally throw up our hands and take hold of His and realize our helplessness without the indwelling of Christ.

The prayer I prayed evoked a gentle reminder from my Father . . . I heard it . . . *"His wife shall be like a fruitful vine about thy house"* . . .

I had always thought this verse referred to fruitful as in "child-bearing", and it may have those connotations. But today I saw something else: a fruitful vine is something out of which fruit grows and flourishes and abounds. The power of my position as a wife and mother is *life-giving* nourishment to my family! Or, it can mean death if the Life-Giver is not pouring through me.

That's heavy! But we all know it's true.

I am to be the vine—the lifeblood of the fruit that God wants to produce in our home. Does my husband flourish or wilt from my influence? Do my children grow and mature or do they shrivel under a harsh spirit?

Oh, ladies, our role is so crucial and what's more, our dependence on the God who placed us here is even more so.

Run to Him each morning, each moment, and beg for His mercy and wisdom and spirit. Meet with Him when you wake up and commit your words, your thoughts—your whole day to Him.

"Faithful is He who called you who also will do it."

The Ministry of Mother

"Mommy, can I have a cup of cold water?"

She's precise like that, my three-year-old, and cute as it is, sometimes her simple request can get lost in the others, in the chorus of children calling my name.

Sometimes I'm tired and the chorus is more of a cacophony; and I don't hear it. I don't hear the Savior's words . . .

> "And whosoever shall give to drink unto one of these little ones even a cup of cold water in the name of a disciple, truly I say unto you, he shall not lose his reward." (Matthew 10:42)

The smallest service, the tiniest act of love is seen and cherished and rewarded by the Sovereign of the universe!

"But I want to do something great for the Kingdom", we say, even if only in our hearts.

How easily we forget . . .

"Whoever wants to be first must be last of all and servant of all." Then he took a little child and put it among them; and taking it in his arms, he said to them, "Whoever welcomes one such child in my name welcomes me, and whoever welcomes me welcomes not me but the one who sent me."

The next time I'll hear Him in my daughter's voice. I'll not fulfill her request out of a desire to simply make it stop. I'll serve her, in love, in the name of the One who has called me to this important ministry—mothering these little ones.

His accolades are enough.

Survival Tips

Sometimes the days are difficult, or circumstances in life become heavy and make motherhood feel impossible. It is those days we must regroup and find real, practical coping strategies to get us to the other side. I pray the following "survival tips" will bring some freedom and ease to your work and help you keep the right perspective until the journey gets easier.

Survival Tip #1

"In survival mode, it's relationship first. All else can catch up later.Cancel as many "extra" activities during the difficult seasons. You are a mother and wife first. If you are struggling to do that well, you are not obligated to add other things to your list. Use discretion and utilize "no" if you have to."

Survival Tip #2

Read. Read out loud, give your children reading challenges, ask an older child to read to the younger ones. Allow them to make "reading forts", go outside and read, etc. Reading is always productive, and it's an easy thing to do when you're feeling tired or low. You may try letting some of your children act out what is being read for added variety and fun.

SURVIVAL TIP #3

Have a bed party. Particularly if you aren't feeling well but you still want to stay close to your little ones, invite them to pile on the bed with you. Bring books, toys (snacks if you're brave) and just enjoy being together, listening to them and laughing with them.

SURVIVAL TIP #4

Do the next thing. Simple as it is, it's a powerful antidote to feeling overwhelmed. Pick one chore, if that's all you feel you can accomplish in a day, and knock it out. The sense of finishing a task will boost your morale.

SURVIVAL TIP #5

Divert the conversation. If the moods seem to be sour, divert attention by announcing something like, *"Okay . . . Susie, tell everyone something you love about your brother."* This usually makes them giggle and then everyone wants a turn. I did this last night at the dinner table when a few of them were irritable, and it worked like a charm.

SURVIVAL TIP #6

Forts can be a great spirit-lifter and fun way for the children to spend an afternoon, particularly on hot days when going out doesn't excite them. Encourage an older child to help with the building and then a read-aloud with some snacks.

SURVIVAL TIP #7

Turn on some music. Music can have a calming effect on frazzled nerves and can bring much-needed distraction.

SURVIVAL TIP #8

Load up and change the scenery. Sometimes cabin fever is all that's making life feel a little more challenging. Go to the park and play with your kids. Fresh air and fun is good for the soul and body.

SURVIVAL TIP #9

Don't be afraid to use some practical, time-saving strategies during difficult seasons. Paper plates, simpler meals (soups, pizza, etc.),

SURVIVAL TIP #10

Survival mode is only for a season, even if it seems to happen a lot at your house. I have good friends who remind me that even the noise and messes of a large family will be sorely missed one day. Soak in the moments—survive them. You will be okay and they will too. Surviving together could be one of the most bonding experiences life has to offer.

About the Author

KELLY CRAWFORD is a Christian, wife, mom and blogger. Her online pseudonym is "Word Warrior" because she seeks to fight with words the cultural lies that are destroying families and homes. She and her husband, Aaron, live with their nine children in the deep South, clinging to a simpler life. Kelly has been seeking to encourage women at her blog, Generation Cedar, for almost six years, where she also runs a cottage industry selling family resources and her homemade skin products (a business born out of adversity). She has been featured in various magazine publications, web sites and interviewed on several radio programs, including Kevin Swanson's "Generations With Vision", speaking on the subject of family enterprise.

Kelly and her family experienced devastating loss in 2011, when an F-5 tornado ripped through their homestead and community. You can read more about their faith through the storm on her website, www.GenerationCedar.com.

Made in the USA
Lexington, KY
13 August 2013